TEAMWORK
SAVES T

Dennis Fertig
Illustrated by Joel Rowe

Rigby®
A Harcourt Achieve Imprint

www.Rigby.com
1-800-531-5015

The Rochette family ate cereal for breakfast every morning. Gabriel liked to read the cereal box. He always checked the box top, too. The cereal company printed points on the box top. Gabriel was saving points to get a soccer T-shirt.

Gabriel's sister Denise liked a different cereal. She was saving the points on her box tops to get music CDs.

Mom and Dad ate Grain Flakes, a cereal for grown-ups. Their cereal also had points on the box tops. They could buy bus tickets with these points.

Gabriel and Denise were students at Elmwood School. One day, the principal had good news. The school band was picked to play in a Memorial Day concert in New York City.

There was some bad news, too. The band would need to take a bus, and that would cost a lot. Elmwood School could not afford to send the band.

Gabriel wasn't in the band, but he thought about the problem. Suddenly, he had an idea. "Let's start a Cereal Points Club."

"I get it," said Denise. "We'll collect points from cereal box tops to get bus tickets for the band."

"That's a great idea, Gabe!" said Lee Park, Gabriel's best friend.

Everyone helped. Students brought in all the cereal box tops that they had been saving. Soon the club had collected six bags of box tops.

The club members counted the box tops. They found that they had enough points to get T-shirts and music CDs, but they didn't have enough Grain Flakes points for even one bus ticket.

"I can't believe we didn't get more Grain Flakes points," said Denise.

"I think that we forgot to say that we needed only Grain Flakes points," said Gabriel.

Lee had an idea. "Let's see if people will trade their Grain Flakes points for the points that we don't need."

The next day, club members made posters.

The club put posters up in the library, movie theaters, and stores.

Cereal Points Club!

Send the Elmwood School Band to New York City!
Trade your Grain Flakes points to get T-shirts and music CDs.

Call the Elmwood School for details. 555-7247

Soon the club was trading points with a lot of people. And these people were mailing their new points to cereal companies for T-shirts and music CDs.

Three weeks later, the club still had only enough bus points to send five band members to New York City.

"I don't think that this is going to work," Gabriel told Mom.

This time Mom had a good idea.

Mom and Dad phoned radio stations, TV stations, and the newspaper. They talked about what the Cereal Points Club was trying to do.

Almost everyone heard the story. Soon the club had bags and bags of Grain Flakes box tops, but it was still not enough.

Now Lee had a great idea. He called the company that makes Grain Flakes. He told them what the Cereal Points Club was trying to do.

The president of the Grain Flakes company was proud of the students for working together. He gave bus tickets to all the members of the Elmwood School Band, because he knew that they had worked so hard.

That's how the Elmwood School Band went to New York City and played in the Memorial Day concert. Teamwork saved the day!